MAGPIE WORDS

KIND SIRS I COULD NOT TELL

IT ALL BUT EVERY WORD IS TRUE

MAGPIE WORDS

SELECTED POEMS 1970-2000

Richard Caddel

WEST HOUSE BOOKS · 2002

Published by
West House Books, 40 Crescent Road
Nether Edge, Sheffield s7 1hn

Distributed in usa by
spd, 1341 Seventh Street
Berkeley ca 94710 - 1409

Text © Richard Caddel 2002
Cover design & origination © Anthony Flowers 2002

Typeset in Jenson at Five Seasons Press, Herefordshire
and printed on Five Seasons one hundred per cent
recycled book paper by Biddles Ltd, Guildford

isbn 1 904052 03 7

These poems are for Ann and Lucy

Contents

Preface   11

Against Numerology   15
A Short Climate-Atlas Of The Soul   18
Baby Days (For Tom, with a cough)   23
Baltic Coast   24
Border Ballads   30
Counter   34
'Darknesse and light...'   39
Early Morning   40
Enchanter's Nightshade   41
Fantasia in the English Choral Tradition   42
Flock   50
For Kosovo: After Alcuin on the Sacking of Lindisfarne   52
For The Fallen   54
For Tom   90
From Wreay Churchyard   91
Gatekeeper, arrowhead...   92
Going Home   93
Ground   94
Larksong Signal   102
Messenger   103
Milkwort   104
Motive   105
Nine Englynion   106
Parsley   108
Poem For My Mother   109
Ramsons   111
Rigmarole: And Each Several Chamber Bless   112
Rigmarole: A Struck Bell   115
Rigmarole: Block Quilt   118
Rigmarole: Night-Driving in Corrèze   122
Rigmarole: The Dogs of Vilnius   126
Rigmarole: Uncertain Time   132

Shelter	135
Smithy	142
Sweet Cicely	143
The Feet of Dafydd ap Gwilym Tapping to the Triads of Dr. Williams	150
The Paths	152
Three Reels	153
Two Movements Which Begin at the Head and End at the Feet	155
Uncertain Steps	157
Underwriter	159
Vers Nègre	170
Writing In The Dark	171
Wyatt's Dream	178
Notes and Acknowledgements	179

Preface

I STARTED READING AND WRITING POEMS for the excitement of the physical impact of words joined together (though I doubt I'd have named it so then) and when that ceases to surprise and amaze me, to be a path of discovery, I'll stop. This selection spans thirty years of work, but it is self-evidently not intended to be a chronology of that process. The chronological approach, whilst of potential interest to a psychoanalyst, has I think little appeal to a notional 'general reader' of poems such as I've always optimistically envisaged as my ideal audience. Instead I've adopted a sequencing device which affords each of these poems a chance to make its own relationships with its readers, and with its neighbours. I was delighted to find that this approach brings to light too many examples of synergy and interaction—*sound sense*—between the poems to be dismissed as 'mere' chance.

There are substantial advantages to a literary career which has been without exception at some distance from that which a friend has engagingly called 'High Street Poetry'. I have at no time been under pressure to produce what I didn't want to, or to work at a pace other than that which allows deliberation and care. Nor have I felt the need to 'write down' to any (real or imagined) marketplace. If there are mistakes, clumsinesses or—heaven help us—*difficulties* in what follows, they are of my own making, and they are there because I wanted them that way. A minimum of notes is provided, usually to introduce compositional approaches which may not be common, but plenty of scope remains for the enthusiastic annotator. Reading the poems out loud will get round most of the tricky bits, I've always found, and certainly makes the process more enjoyable.

I have been abnormally lucky in having, from the start, a small core of listeners—family and friends—whose support has been steadfast. Their speech is in turn embedded in these pages, alongside the other (printed or sounded) source material which has sustained me over the years. There are also, out there, a small number of dogged and independent readers who have, at different times, signalled their interest and approval from afar. This collection is offered to such brave spirits, in friendship. A host of others deserve direct thanks, and many are acknowledged at the back of this book—but above all, on this occasion, special thanks go to my present editor and publisher, Alan Halsey, for his ready help and encouragement throughout this project, and to my wife and daughter, for their own particular brands of long term support and encouragement, and for putting up with more than their shares of writer's grumps. I couldn't have done this without them.

Richard Caddel
Durham June 2001

MAGPIES or pies might be called poets, because they can speak words with different sounds [...]. The sound of its voice may mean either the loquacity of heretics or the discussion of philosophers.

Anonymous C.13th bestiary, MS Bodley 764, trans. Richard Barber

Against Numerology

(i) — if you spill salt, throw a little over your shoulder, for memory

It's freezing and you try to remember June,
the garishness and wonder. Or else a song
you loved when you were young, and now
it's stale. Faces you saw in lino, little houses
they told you weren't true but they were, they
were: not the thing itself but the sense
of other and contrary things is real.

(ii) — the whitebeams

The weather down the dales.
Then they were so hungry that they struck
and kept striking. The berries
turning scarlet in the sun, the leaves,
the leaves streamed out like banners.
When they drank it was so hard
and earnest, you'd think they'd never stop.

(iii) — fighting for strangers

The decision was endorsed by committee. Ask
if my attitude is morally defensible. Ask me
if I loved you then. Now look into the black trees
dividing sky in little chunks, a strike force, a
shanty where small, idiot hungers pipe — where,
in the world, look, another cloud gone down, and
more investment would cost you an eye and ear.

(iv)—*nulla rosa est*

For everything you ever had stays with you
like a Japanese garden, raked sand. For
folk songs are the souls of dead workers.
For the grove we met in had seven black trees
like banners, and seven is a forgotten number. For
if you lost someone you must hug their absence.
For the other half of this verse is missing.

(v)—*seagulls are the souls of dead sailors*

Pull it down like a white hankie, its
anger in bedrooms, in windowframes,
fearful to be alone in its night.
Cry to wake the dead—blade
across sky, the banners legend on the wind
tossed out to sea—remember the sea
was always in your eyes on waking.

(vi)—*lowlands (for Ann)*

Figures dancing a long way off on hills, a
dream we wandered in too freely. Waking
to long for the quiet marshy levels, salt
sea wind in our hair and the moon. Rain
in tiny shells had washed sleep from our eyes,
we cried, as if the songs had never been,
as if our weed filled hearts were cragfast still.

(vii)—the shaggy inkcaps

Autumn—before I noticed, you were gone—
like a little home dissolving on itself.
To know that loss: the pain of hunger
and of love, and in clear air
the acrid smell of bonfires. And to know
I'll find you again, soon. Each day now
I leave the house as if I'll never return.

A Short Climate-Atlas Of The Soul

snow sleet and hail

Vapour
snow
crystals
the same
        winter but hail
        rising columns

      crystals falling
    droplets moving
crystals building

strong
down through
until they fall

magnified

you see
you see
you see

why does it rain?

     even
simple
    vapour
   droplets
    are visible
   together

   air
falls as light

    you wish
    you wish

One swallow. What can this bird be doing behind by itself? Why might not they have all staid, since this individual bird seems brisk, & vigorous.

air is warm

    and so rises

⨳

north south east and west winds

    tops a church
               design
    they point to
    they are really
    only tells
    only tells

    hard and fast
    usually closed

    Grey, windy, soft & agreeable.

    the wind is like
    the way from
    the south

weather sayings

Handed down
        predictions
of today

see about
the big picture

   perhaps
a red sky
with this
there is
Swithins

(Bestowed great waterings in the garden.)

animals
change
on their

petals

prevailing winds

A wind
        direction
trying to prevail

The bat is out. Beetles hum.

westerly wind
if you were
of the wind
that blew

if you look
especially
leaning

———

you sleep
you sleep
you sleep

Baby Days
*(for Tom
with a cough)*

Rocks
and sea-harbours

burning. Slow tide
tugging the shore—

the old song, a man
is turning over
pebbles /
        in his hand—

capsized days
days drunk as glass

fill the bosun's lamp
with compassion:

the beach, our love, illness.

Baltic Coast
for Lauri and Liisi

'our books, our memories, ourselves'
— Jaan Kaplinski

BALTIC COAST I : VAIM

very simple: you
mishear *coast*

for *soul*   from which
we strike out

each morning   milfoil words
at the path's edge

Autumn mists
a few herbs

round the house
you walk from town

towards the shore
and are lost

    ceaselessly   without
    rest   forever

BALTIC COAST II : GULF

light arcs on the gulf   a haze
       our words caught forever
       in the present—shoreline
gleam with pines   maps with boatways
       altered made wrong and
       waste slick pumped to sick sea.

All power decays in its own hands.
       Watch a smoke pile
       drifting
black to north   *a raft*
       of tolerance   along the margins of
           late evenings sky

on estuaries   generous mind
       facing our days in bright air

BALTIC COAST III : MARGINAL

       dancing
       folding

       mumbling
       knowing

       watching
       eating

    breathing
    hoping

    queuing
    growing

    lightening
    meeting

        raining
        leaving

BALTIC COAST IV : THREAP

for Eric Mottram

on heathland
in failing light
'the quail whistles
and who attends'

dark trees fold in
around steep slab rooves
tied to a stake
an old cow calls

allegiances never taken
lightly   no friendship
left to fend
for itself: noun, local:

persist in asserting; affirm;
maintain obstinately or aggressively

BALTIC COAST V : 'WHO ARE THE REAL ESTONIANS?'

too many onions and too much salt
definitely too much beer

I've failed my language and ideology test
I probably sing and dance too much

soon my mental workforce will be halved
in line with western economies

too many russians and barbie dolls
the hot water clunks and runs cold

nobody believes in the politics
I've kept to my self too long

I'm still found out drunk
on the streets too late

each morning I wake
and you seem further away from me

BALTIC COAST VI : CONTINUOUS PRESENT
for Jaan Kaplinski

lakes and woods and
        maggots in apples
small blue

        flower by the
path   towards darkness
        a long man

tethers his cow
        the forest
swallows him   shortages of

        'semolina, socks
underwear and alcohol'
        always here   always

anywhere   always going we
        know not where

BALTIC COAST CODA : CHILDREN DANCING

because you won't
hang out a witch charm
the skies will become
neither blue nor grey

amber! amber and charred
sticks on that shore
whose seas have lost their clarity
for ever

Border Ballads

littoral

I gave my love a phoneme
    to send her on a journey
I gave her a sentence
    before we crossed

I drew my love towards me
    down by the water
I caught my breath sharply
    as we waited on the strand

down by the shoreline
    I lost all my language
deep in the margins
    my words deserted me

speech became a stranger
    and waves closed behind us
and home had no meaning
    and mist obscured our passage
and day was dark as night

the bell-betrayal

Voice—sounding all parts
turning in silence ground
struggling by dozy riverbeds
lolling towards return
      metal cast in a deep pool

In dark inherent memory
digging these lousy borders
breath moving within us
trust in tides to return
      metal cast in a deep pool

the little girl burned

The sun dropped
a crystal hate speech
crying on the moorside

Where worlds meet
bounden all in the bloodstream
crying on the moorside

Crying on the moorside

silk tie

What we could buy—
child in the treetops
          ashtree and garden fork

brittle shell falling from
that high brightness
          redshank and wrack

As if turned by wind's edge
lapping fallible banker
          bond and silk hankie

in trade night against
silence stone standing
          ashtree and garden fork
          starlight and tides

ghost dance

cornish   livonian   seminole creek
etruscan   panoba   pipil
eyak   dalmatian   tasmanian   breton
pawnee   nicolena   manx   ugong

feering fresian   huron   dyirbal   khoi
cayuga   gothic   yahi
lenca   east sutherland gaelic   wapo
kamu   dakota   pictish   san

bastle

Song worn to a bleached stone
story we dream alone—
After my death, what is my colour?
        a sea speech remembered

A little wall eye cloud across sun
'a little rushlight'—words
could change everything
        a sea speech remembered

Counter

> *Kardang garro*
> *Mammul garro*
> *Mela nadjo*
> *Nunga broo*
> — Stefan Themerson

> *+ + + + + The sound, the proper*
> *Voice for the saying, the murmuring, the uttering, the chant*
> *Of wheat and barley changed by murmur into animal liveliness,*
> *By uttering, by striking the stomach and opening the . . .*
> — Armand Schwerner

white for white — an air beyond crossmatch —

Living out on contrary margins
you tell them everything, a
boundary of your resistance, a
song, like an old charm
simply a pattern on air

— red — brown — magenta —

they boil in June evening dancing
aside from their veins
markers of fast lane memory and
living purpose in colour, sharp
observed natures of common flowers
subdividing our cellular carriers

O WITH US AND
NOT-WITH US,
JOIN
THIS LAMENT

—orange—vermilion—yellow—black—

Watching
    stars—
their great
    mercy
stillness,
   so that
in our
   distant
watches we
    become
for a moment
    together

unending

wasted lyric in sickness
our words gone from us into that chimney
mistake, imagining a singing loss so that a
creature down and miles out of
things for the lack of which the
world dies daily

—green—black—yellow—cream—

into a compound vision dance
of white optic—too much
white clogging the bee
dance step
stem cell leap—swifts shriek asleep
allergenic
on wing over some distance ahead

> O WITH US
> AND NOT-WITH US,
> JOIN
> THIS PRAYER

—black—blue—yellow—

    People at night.

    Turning

    & breathing. Turning

    &

    breathing. Tur-

ning & loving

            brea-

thing.

        Turning

    & breathing.

chimney sound system through which
these parts push towards
a crossmatch—agile
out of the tribe-song so
moved, a token
pollen-bearing form struggling
alone in its channels

—*brown*—*black*—*yellow*—*crimson*—

on creature out of IV drip given finding
on bone in warm clonal expansion
completely to hills and water
out of a grace I counter

—*orange*—*blue*—*yellow*—*white*—

    Wind
           makes
  leaves

        fall
  but fall
        is not

  what they
        do, dancing
so—it is

        an active
  process still
          unending

           flexible
                     response
        to air

deliberate violation, poison
leaked to tissue—
or across borders—deliberate
form seeking in fleet
foot dance, a signal
towards an unknown

                                      O WITH US
                                      AND NOT-WITH
                                      US, JOIN
                                      THIS PRAISE

—thus night—shadow—purple—

*'Darknesse and light
divide
the course of time'*

grey coat
grey eyes
ellipse of morning
pebble dash sea

Early morning: train horn signal
a minor third downline
a bird sings, there's nothing
on my mind.

Enchanter's Nightshade
homage to Louis Zukofsky

Circe a lute she on—you say
could risk your lot on a grace
family this music—come buy us
in shady places and chant
at night's hades not bitter
sweet toothed leaf is hearts cling
not a trope a white flower is
scarcely noticed song stem so long

Fantasia in the English Choral Tradition

signals :
        pact or parts
corresponding
             in January
bonfires smoke
down the river bank
            a way off—

moving (lunchtime)
                out of the realm of
false, muddled argument
                  into that contact
with the world in which
              (for which)
I live—
      to point towards—
because there is no 'away'
                to sling things to
and to live here
          is not to escape

—you feel the heat
                —centres of learning
            everything
            tumbling
and still
        that 'human record'
how many million years
              complete.

a voice perhaps
            (active)
wavered as it spoke

                        bird in flight
but held its point
you out there
            violin parts
              (tail feathers)
twine and cross over
                        was it
chance brought us
silent, dark
            and now with these
small voices
            (elements)
accords

⚔

silent and dark
            as knowledge
till we catch that flash—
white tail feathers—
                        red gash underwing
like stored fruit
wavered, but held true
                        one winter's day
recalled, spark
            that took the fire
that gave the heat
            loom of lighthouse
in black night
            inside
a comforting fire to warm the hall
                                    outside
the winter storms raging
                    the bird
passed in a flash
            into the dark
of which we know nothing

                                    that instant
—the voices—
lines climbing, over-
                    lapping and
climbing into the air—
skylarks over any downland
                                        signals to
(according with)
                    the other, the
strong insistent line
of memory
                gone downwards
into earth

⚹

something reaching out to you
                                    direct
from birdsong
                from the warmth
of two people together
                            for an instant
different from any other—
to wait perhaps a life
                        for as much—
lighthouse puts out its signals
to no ships
            but sings
a voice of life
                how small it may seem
in the dark
                how far its bonfire heat
may carry
            as traces from Koobi Fora
for millions of years like yesterday
for so long
                has envy, worry,

    kindness
              been established. The hard
reality—and here
                 I go soft
on a bonfire
in no time

⚘

                                   (weardale section)

lost in everyday deposits
of bedrock
            clouds bent in huge mass
as swirling lava long ago borne down
currents drifting
              signalling   granite sharp
in mineral air
everyday we share
            cumulus over
giant blocks of earth
rock laid down under what pressure
                      trees
nodding and turning bent down
under wind mass
heat meeting cold

and the people moving in slow giant eddies
like a great dance   like cloud spray
upon the face of the earth
                which had supported them
over the ores of the earth
                which had supported them
the people with wit and love and tiredness
and humour
            like granite
alive and moving
              under the clouds
over the face of earth

⚘

because there is no away to sling to
(turning radar dish over
may trees exploding blossom)
these fragments come
                        bounding
out of time
        to call to
the heat of the world
                        of which
we are part
        against loneliness
a pact held in
the need of leaves
                to move
together
        their swell like the seas
the deeper
        downhill further and
darker and the
wilder higher reaching
                      to the sky
rejoicing

as to make it simple
                    and of sympathy
new

it is raining very hard
it is warm
the birds are   (plainly)
    loving it

whatever it is

      dealing with the anger of a friend
            in the cool evening
      dealing with the anger of a friend
            with a breeze lifting the treetops
            in the late twentieth century
      dealing with the anger of a friend
            and against all hate and cruelty
            when the birds have roosted
            hearing my footsteps on tarmac
            watching a cow blink
            while the earth is being defoliated
      dealing with the anger of a friend
            as clouds scud across the stars
      dealing with the anger of a friend
            in the darkened room
      dealing with the anger of a friend
            while it's still moist from rain
            trying to help
      dealing with the anger of a friend
            hearing a car go down the hill
            and the grass pushing up pavements
            streetlamps in islamic patterns
      dealing with the anger of a friend
            as the flowers grow

    ※

dealing with a cow blink pushing up the darkened room   a car moist trying to grow   the birds lifting the tarmac as the clouds in islamic patterns   hearing my anger scud across the stars   the flowers   the century roosted late   a friend defoliated in the cool evening in the darkened room   hearing the earth blink   the grass still moist from hate   dealing with a friends cow   a car   anger   blink in the moist evening   trying to help the flowers in the darkened room

hoping for a light to steer by but not touch

    ※

(redesdale section)

lighthouse out there
                insistent
loom seen off the land
loom
     of a city seen in the hills at night
signals over space
              in the night
where you are

or striding over turf
                the children
learning to catch things
                and let them go
and I struggle for breath
for plant names

  ⚐

to recall
      those who are expert on apple trees
the trick being
       to love
anything
(a bonfire, a bird's tail
              in flight)
              to start with
a point
     to correlate with
it's important
       to make mistakes
in a way, once
       in a way
parsley
     reaching for the measure
the song wavered   recalling
     evening
   smell of parsley

       thinned in late may after rain
                              turning
over and over
              air shifting over ground
violin,   skylarks wilder
                        reaching out
by the stone house
trees bent under wind
                        standing out
years   above a river
of years   (memory)
in which there is no rest
                        song lapping
its banks at night
                when the owls call
drift down like clouds
                    like rock
and we to each other calling
our wary friendship

there is too much
                  to want
to want to lose
               of song (breath)
of heat   of light
                    passing wonderful
lending radiance

I am back in thought
                    in the hills
with scope
        to sing
the things I love
            as they occur
this instant

everyday

Flock

Denied it. Said that he'd
    not been told
the guidelines altered
    over his

signature. Frost upon grass
    waving in
morning light. That paper
    missing from

the files, tests showing it had
    been taken.
To walk across such hills
    with a song

somewhere behind the back
    of the brain
and no ache. Not arms, but
    equipment—

so that full details need not be
    released. When
these documents were made public
    it was thought

better not to respond. The heart
    pounded on
turf, birdsong, light cloud
    on the wind

and direction not important.
    Told it was
safe—business wanted the
    orders, they

were cleared, the vessel sailing
    west outside
the zone. Atmosphere up here
    so clear, a

shock on the chest and a joy
    to the heart.
And as yet no minister or director
    has resigned

over it. *What delectable mountains*
    are those? And
whose be the sheep that feed
    upon them?

For Kosovo
After Alcuin on the Sacking of Lindisfarne

Our fields we leave waste
earth bankrupt
in pain for children lost
to stealth and bad faith

Ruled by chance and death
each in our time
denied our grief, no privacy
in this brute casual world

Homes desolate, shamed,
memories broken, frailty
questioning what
can't be known

Perhaps elsewhere there's peace
—but not here, lost, lost in
this world's
swirling tides forever

Laid low who once was free
in rags who once was proud
eyes dim who once was clear
weak, famished who once was strong

A small voice by your ear
clear as a trumpet
as we turn
sick from the burning world

And so we change
and so everything moves on
and so what remains elsewhere is
uninterrupted day

For The Fallen: A Reading of Y Gododdin

Part I

1

I claim
in the
song
place
not
from
doorway
one
earth
poetry is now parted

2

in
of
shift
under
light
fleet on
blue
worked gold
shall not be
between
shall
song
field
than
quicker
than
friend was
wrong
in what land
son

3

went
breathless
shattered
as many
not retreat
cut
floor
before
but one

4

wearing a
swoop
that was
not set
before
the land
neither
no-one
against

5

wearing a brooch
amber
in return for
down
Northern
      planning
        would be shattered

6

in fury
his death
before
fell before
fell
in one hour
quicker
quicker
before
in return
will be

7

laughter
harsh array
calm
to do
old and young
meeting

8

eager laughter
savage
without much noise
giving

9

Catterick
feast
fighting
there was silence
though
certain

10

went to
would be
great dark blue
close ranks
have
spared
friend lost
to leave
no father
son

11

dawn
their fears
charged
stains
valiant
before

12

Catterick dawn
shortened
drank
for a year
may their
white
before

13

with the day
shame
inevitable

blades
speak
for his
stood
splendid

14

went to
greedily
lament
fiery
      there rushed
      no great
           intent
      none
      from the
           scattered
land
without
long
memory
of his people
place

15

went
on his land
collected
loud thunder
champion
tore and cut
above
the harsh
humbled
before

16

of the land
fell
fought for
with
long
fate
was for
drank
bitterness

17

from
followed
feather
drinking
came
gold
ran under
sound
a bear

18

front
sunlight on grass
found
island
ford
with his
drinking
hall of
grandeur
was
strong wine

reaper
sweet
purpose
leeks
bright
sang a song
in
winged
not solid
fell
in the
cry
without fail
fury
the green earth
mighty

19

right
stain
fifty
hounds and
three
gold
three
three gold
three
three
leaping
harshly
three
easily
gold
three
sprang
and

of
crafty
ask
from
better than
serpent / path

20

wine
  were many
  clash
    ford
rushed rose
  green
shattered
  the tearer
  down
    broke
son
  sold his life
  for the
    with
both
pledge
  brought
  brave
    he charged

21

wine / hall
border region
was the
everyone
blood
years
vastly
talk of the world

22

they were
vessels
for a year
three
drink
three
two
song

23

pleasure
harsh
drink
with blows
he was
do not tell
anyone

24

borderland
gold
bright
protected
nature
only son
do not tell
harsher

25

amid
England
east
widows
pen

26

grey movement
afire
radiant
food
left at
dew-fall
wave
poets
deprived
before
      in his
blood
son

27

unremembered
left no
did not leave
new years day
his land
generous
in the
conflict

28

true as
horses
cast
wide
was not
fierce
threw
steaming
lovable
and savage
as a reaper
to flow

29

southern
sea
      modestly
       drinking
there was
never
mothers
son

30

lovable
seized
gentle
     of
songs
of home

31

lovable
fighter
gold
shattered
furious
kept
grief
purposefully
may he be
in full

32

into
a wild boar
bull
wolves
witness
and and
from
from before
after
his father

33

leaping
clarified
in
feast
and
and
steel
in the fight
slain
homeland

34

together
a year
sad
no mothers son
lasting
after
spirit
and costly
land

35

cry
blue
sharp
and shining
cut
fire
gold
and handsome

36

never
great
fiery
he would not make
fame
resounded
rock of
son of

37

never
except / son
manner
son
fire
he was
before
        stress
bitter
man

38

never
graces
truly
struck
pointed
through
horses racing
in the day of
green dawn

39

never
        so noble
finest
refuge
prince
I have seen
        arms
sharpest
like rushes
I will sing
        praise

Part II

40

he gainsaid his room in the house front
defies odds common and odds even
anyways around—rifle-certain
who'd ever a road in lower elfin
everywhere folded and moor grey tarnished

41

he gangwayed for room in a nice town
worth more in a hunters wired wing
eased aloft nor rang clay to finish
adders-hog far and not ragged other
everywhere folded and moor grey tarnished

42

disengaged in a room rag drying aloft
canny big he grew and hurried me gaff
going on and on with meaning rid way off
against fooldog with heart enough
anything folded my bonny moorhen

43

men cormorant in atheist cunning
win faith amid faith earthen
      O ancient hand me down
      handcuffed cum ruinous
           O golly gosh going round
    like thunder
    so long Dario my
          rag runaway thinning

44

disc inside a room rag drains off cowards
we rescue layers of shipyard men
and it goes through the rough blurting bloodless
narrows each way—fine feasting star
and delight gone loud to your candleman
go forth warily ruth run to each doorchime
truth go run amok I'm lain astrew stairway
telling of worthy dove gored
angel with highness bid artless in mind
      of cronies aged way over
caravan roaring a cloud clod avower
no shame to those who baulk at clause four

45

I'm droning dreary and dry
I'm loose and I'm this-ways walking
I'm widow-wilt in your head
I am wire eagle with them
with news along the way then
dulled duelled and broken
amid more yen
when was Merlin a courteous pen
price in words was a shallow shaman
try where a big gun was brandished
during when and why my son went

46

I'm droning dreary and dry
when in the ear wider and wanting
is ariel clear and full amber
in England's tertian rag trenchant unbent
how shall we man blades Hebron to Tuzla
      known wishing in island
O gallant wit and asking
trailing and dying he went

47

aura for care
crystal worth clear
not adept fore-by
or them with nailed clay
      odd in lunch laughing
not drawn Gododdin their plain gear
nor by cuneiform cunning words

48

pan across frost to cuneiform cloud
in iron wind we wisen gathered
to heather ankle with rhythmic wire nod
O the door the actor wire core thin dry
O manners with oiled day churchy eye
O the dinners feeding secretly
kneel with the wine fed men not by

49

not with vinegar plain
not high loaf or thin
not war that hurting
or the dread raining
on eastern England
gathering the hay in
and bending for new land
O faith of fuelling
O Catterick wherein
miner Aneurin
is wired to a lesson
over Wear running
new chant Gododdin
by Wear deep dialling

50

growl it at jugulars wired and goring
clary for her lesson is encircled
not on the dear mum not mouthing
more ironing to get on her gathering
O North so clever and clear in harming
O harsher and war doers' undoing
see now that clause four they've forged

51

not of bodywork causing senility
      I listen lawn mown
go the lay gaily if guarded
go the lay lady or rifle
before the line we saw our flesh
rags budding deeper and browner
gnawed in a new-age face fair
wire of a worm-search
crying all heralds of law
acrid eyelid-briar sown
grain and unhidden forehead
they search and search harder
warrior not often rich dread of
hailing a hubris pub row

52

a grin I alone have
a wry burning train track truth
core I fancy I'm gore of a banker
busies in brash brawling bar
amble amidst air amidst earth
amble in reading in rich words
his brows bright trailing rice on roadies
no way he gave way in eagerly
not angry or one-way into the old ways

53

no man warned or gloried
or kin well garnered
no man thuds mirthwards
a fresher mime-clue
chill a bloodier chill
chiller the bell
in may dew upon the chill
in corner angles
blush—bush of the law
and a poet in amber

54

ditherful add-on in additives
annually bad when nailed laddered clustered
no morning in wrath and lord
nor shed waste nor aether in china
is gone—thrum the penner
new-laid in orchard more march again
who laden in rotten earth of Saxon

55

queue a rain cedar far-flung
who could in one fired gyre chastened
byre or hurdle hair or head or current
some complaint on loggers or leather scent
ogre freezeth rageth witty and nascent
lover mam I dig and a home to rent

56

O winter and mead thirst in aether gaining
clue rig Orion—news going late letting
come clueless O least in view
rag Catterick holds faith and clue
on gorse muddy fog flower dew
O drew chant naming in anger the few

57

O wine faith and moth faith is grace-sent
wire in rest molest a nest thick went
glow dull and droll and befeathered
going amidst a maul or muck scent
on gorse my dog-hard life and falling
or rue it at college in wired garage
O dry chant reality's grey sound at Catterick
true naming one wire and not cursing

58

who bid the young highwire in parent
        made peel awry he
who'd bid thy own ivy a tree
who'd among old or thin
win a maiden hiding
        in highstrung history
and Tom Caddel in catcher flights
marching on trust in moors

59

anger dour dane
sharp stuff we grin
send a worm again
        in lean budding
Arthur in all
drew sad dresser
sent away war
in this cadaver
        inlaws wear none
isle in thick gnaw
newsdesk true and far
led in the dark
        O drydock drink
see where youth wears fire withered

60

    anger doing down
    any scoffing
        in mean bidding
    lead roof lowerer
    in marsh of wire
        rag of cotton
    wrecking of Arthur
    of worrying bath
    Cymric tarred hearth
        a rage of Merlin

61

    anger dire dawn
    serves saffron green
    engage in vain
        inlaid budding
    ariel railway
    trace track chimeways
    in rue coppery
        cordway laying
    choir youth elsewhere the gyres withered
    rector stair-hater more gobsmacked
    tutor tracing air care of the lathe

62

    clan for lead roof
    claw gift aloof
        wrong wreath in morning
    crawler clothier
    lawn feathered
        tidal flight at blest seaman
    loose art too close the
    law in a lather
        since no ideal's a bargain
    see there youth always on highwire raised
    rector tillerman moor pub flyer
    tutor treading air care of the lyre

63

earthly deft songs coming caffeine
in sad ear at Catterick rapidly breaking
brother a year wiser sung
        sung it with a wind
        Dial M for Murder
                O gallant befringed
this drawl kid nowhere a cuff wrecked
coffee coming here to a craft so dared

64

ah the dog gone no common offering
torn tan and thunder a rivering
gored Arthur might marching musty
rough fettle ruffle on either knee
gore going the different dining car
        or main lad in the sky
I whisked awry wrist with a hard folly way
        made wine glow and wide lustre
a wheel I am fed O daily
winefed of wide North son so dearly

65

earthly songs clear or certain
a chime defiant delays Orion
rife scent I lifted pen or ink clued
        in anger glory birds a-living
an arles for many dogs marching mean
of deeds we do our way by the gallon
at Catterick a fresh new door lacking
way they went clothed in sea fog iron
or else a tremor treads galleon
oath I did amongst the bared Britons
Gododdin O bell welling not chiming

66

earthly songs with common refrains
loud lodger-bird by dizzy want
how many in hill bird idle amount
every great march a mead feathering
forgetting the airing when fainting

67

earthly dog songs clear on common
our negus morning fog mistress mine
a match for her dry wonder
old buffer whistling a land of the broken

68

no portent from mauled noise of
ragtime railway train authored
too big for truth truly kindled
Tuesday whistled in clothes dithered
Wednesday butchery is done
Thursday kindly outmoded
Friday calamity closed
Saturday differing yoked wethers
Sunday clans go red adrenal
Monday hide mine eyes wading waylaid
news draws Gododdin wed to the cluttered
rag pebble mad dog pain gored
naming a man O gallant not delayed

69

mock away wraith in moor
in gunnels at peripheral ragstone
      by shores of the Wear
      sing hinnies cold

   avail of the guard
     in degree
but cold hold a minute—but lay
but going a willing journey

70

mock away wraith in morning
pancreas in ruin in mourning
O drawers in houses undiluted
rag song of want guise thing
old gear of goon squad chews wading
malefic booze true-certain
old clue and cladding wears thin
leatherfull dual fighting
   O most wretched
    delayed escape stair
      awful in morning

71

he fell headlong to depth
no delay who with wrenching pen
disgorged brain fuel lads a-going
cunning in rain a stair edger
eastwind kangeroo'd ghastly his going
dilute disdain carefully filling
disgorged pen viburnum bran
fetching march a worn search at each wide dawning
go for it go for gold against disdain

72

air draws a ruddy wiseapple
let gorse away with a fiddle
worth weird words and nervous
search away am I red in faith

singing a search — seeking a song
our fellows cleat daywise and cluttered
penitent enough in neckwear carved
hunt amber but go to penitence

73

faint and hard on the far gale
    and his table is withered
darkly the mode melds a mangle
crisis arguing a league in war
sad loose English leaves a door
wry benefit hid in a guitar
ah wine cluer to achieve
go on and on with faith
safely care away the winners
tear away thin face fast strumming
canker west dear can go west wing
by orphans goddamned breed

74

my thin orthodoxy negates
my motley dog clawhammer
but does a choice on chordway
not odd of wrath gift coffered
muddying onions are we held
not odd are lights born or bothersome
angel where our china lived with
in high flown belayed her belied her a dimwit
godly Sir heron Cliff and law inactive
searching in ignorant highlands
wear freshly by flame hard rag a scarp

75

the far fuel and growing
the lady and the hero
neither overheard nor strumming
neither earth fed nor drumming
nothing we rely on is held
not owed our keys upon the blue
not chilly waster train led to rue
draws to choose cleverer than you

Part III

76

making a music out of language
making a moon
red air flame under stars
yesterdays filled with singing
yesterdays text of today
unreal // distinguish
can words make grief
so good // finding
naming one unchanging and changed

77

O gathered in blue aether
destroyed // in thin air
// a lost language
a power play // paratactic
I away in laughing
truly truth runs the lawns
run good with none better
thrill drunk with each letter

78

a good thing // growing
to be done by morning
crawl amidst gorse and law
growing growing enough
     I miss him much
     run in his words
     in new wood shoots
         in Great High Wood
catching breath to be anew
catching air // catching dew

79

brightness falls from the air
bring drink in the night where
grows a chill // there
queens have died young and fair
caressing // whitely care
against wild flower going bare
a dawn of the odd one where
we dreamed // together share

80

truant love // its games
gone deaf // glow angry
// truant away
winter in dread
long sighing and crying
paper betrayed the land
rueful // ill-led
gorse I trod by glow-worms
dupe held in thought
clear sight on a frosty night

81

gardening trees grow long
sadly falls dew on digging
stabat mater why did he go
      run to nest to fly further
mind growing // leaving slowly
      away ancient //
rather howl a cloisterful afraid
      hand in eyelid a lover lost

82

    alone at the end
    alone lost
    heir of ragweed
    in rough seed
    in the crowsnest
    in the frighteners
    burnt whiteness
    of drunkenness
    and bright talk
    nothing warmed
    in grieving
    in snowstorm
        a story told
    story so eager
    of fair anger
        keener the danger

83

    down I dive
    in deep despair
        fear for him
    with failing breath
    all puffed out
        crying for
    whats lost
    close loved
        under stars
    in Northland

    nobody
        brighter
    if the throes
    of speech pass
        cheerfully
    we think it good

we think we should
        remember //
late at the door
talking with friends
        footstep
shape strumming
        and talking
out of the green decoded
luck won full in short space a
        blues explosion
out on your own kind sea
known to friends and lost

84

diamond eye closed //
dialogue anger in grief
deeper eager go further
// over airwaves
reverend fire running in minds
        let for growing
his dead face // pale
glass turned over and out

85

what pushing out went
not from home //
        tall and rangy
        fair hair falling
            running lightly
all waste // is
eager fierce for searching
        by any side
        by glad forlorn
        by bells ringing
            in lightness

//
where buds go
cunning in breathing
if it comes to living
if it comes to happiness
someone and someone and someone
a change of breathing
came to the great sky reeling
in solo weary red
//
glad as an echo
in bed in the uplands running

86

new dolour ahead of English
no day no departure //
no magic in new labour
no to student hardship
and a single benighted oracular
//
would she go for it // gaily
sing it on the streetcorners

87

true sung to grey
bright // dryeyed
cried aloud why
ahead O voicebeat
a scrawled anthem
true naming one man absent

88

true sing //
forever bright
true singing
guitar group
true sung
a grey glove
dogs true sing
truth not return

89

making a music out of memory
in syntax of daring
in old epic // and tragedy
and dearly spoken
early course wordlessly learned
and conference crashing in
awful loss stars sing in threes
calamity discourse red and away

90

sowing the wood a green branch
      writing sharp as a pen
O search in anger //
      hearing away in the sky
my friend waning into nightfall
      playing a tight lead
dew on the fence freezes
exhaust fumes turn in the air

91

away care on the land // tory and
woe to the rage galactic //
and stuff your social justice
      land in its death throes
cover my arse administrators
gormless // in coverup
away smirch on the glass
of brightness rubbed clean

92

gone over the odds on rhyme
swan white in March searching
in anger // seaweed pulling
an ember called morality
      O gutsy drinker
      at their ghastly parties
      falling laughing
           a runaway green
certainly the speech //
unyielding while breath lasts

93

new face fair as heaven
in faith rocked somewhere else
metal // struck in the air
      never well meant in wielding
never still over // hid unawares
a dream we wandered in too freely

94
//
cloudy
//
//
//
brows

95

lather the moon
in growth too soon
baling out of meaning
yo tenia un hijo
sing of tomorrow
hid by the boiler
welled with pride on earth
can we in waste //
old labour in faith
call out the lads
overthrow sleep enough
overthrow lurid denial
overthrow good old call
alone they fell //
no wiser mumbling
enough away from grief
and gladly to hills
we standing together
gentle farewell

96

trawl Merlin by sea
three strands of white flowers
blow on the worlds bards

97

everyday walking in clear air so thin
        in lean-to tin rain
everyday in love along by the //
everyday steelwork clouds dispersing
everyday box of gone lightly
        he dead under the stars
everyday looking to night sky hoping
everyday absence // back thrown

98

gaily over the mosslawn
into this fairness //
go with ragwort and cinquefoil
tapping our Eden for free
meant for a gaffer at law
        chance kings and desperate men
caring cathedral by // grey play at
        womble muck and sneedball
if only my boy had been a bear
        him roughly treated
// upon earths green mantle
        death be not proud

99

if you want to sing to the moon
if stars appear to hold them
all gone in ever clue golden
go lightly O head //
go sing brain beyond care
        since he wasn't Arthur
rung through and through it
in gallant guitar spreads

100

light on the air he lived
deftly delightful with
a personal speech
    if he was over
      in gracing going
          in falling unselfish
    a bright tight lad
    kind to them all
    ever our loss
         a winner in his words
    all gentle and warm
    wit was unrealised
         when from us he went

For Tom

Dear head, four days ahead of love's day
I bring you love. Not that you lack that,
heart, or music, living far beyond stars
close in our hearts memory and moving

hard as you did then under my hand.
Never still, your humour and sharp mind
returned bright now, little carer. So I
stumble to rest missing you, not twenty.

10/2/96

From Wreay Churchyard

What of memory, a
        film not
wound on properly, cold
        daylight.

Pine trees, then, for
        memory, a
black plastic sheet
        flapping. Pinecones

of stone. Letter B
        stray in the
glass, larksong, fire
        forgotten, it was

Spring in the far
        hills, it was
time.

Gatekeeper, arrowhead
sickener.   Burrow
Mump,
        distributor head.
Matrix-cutter.

Cheddar, limestone, *mare incognitum*.
Tony and Liz, clustered
bellflower
            osiers and
fool's parsley.

Going Home
for John Riley

What in the world we see
is what's important. There
the days seemed shorter and our hearts
spun with the compass under

trees, magnificent pointers
out of galaxies. Continental drift,
an appointment we were late for,
an old friend missed.

Ground
on a theme by E. M. Nicholson

Theme

Throstles feeding
on the ground

stand stiffly upright
head cocked to one side

alert for signs of prey
near the surface

running or hopping
at intervals

for a few feet
to the next listening point

⚹

A dark city road—a few throstles feeding
and a street cleaner's brush banging on the ground

in the early fifties—streetlamps stand stiffly upright
gleaming in morning. The cleaner's head cocked to one side

listening to a policecar cruising, alert for signs of prey
in dark sidestreets. And townsfolk hover near the surface

of sleep, their children running or hopping in dreams
of flight and pursuit, to wake at intervals

to grey dawn. The cleaner works on for a few feet
towards the next listening point of that bird-ridden time.

⚹

Our wild hearts! Who knows what song the angels sang?
   'Circles and right lines limit and close all bodies
and the mortal right-lined circle must conclude
     and shut up all.' *As the wind blows, and we are lost in it.*

Throstles feeding on the ground stand stiffly upright
    head cocked to one side, alert for signs of prey
near the surface, running or hopping at intervals
    for a few feet to the next listening point.

⚹

July—and still damp after much rain,
   throstles feeding on the ground
     as though their lives depended on it.

The garden—a painted biscuit-tin-lid, hollyhocks
   stand stiffly upright, heads cocked to one side—
     listening, as we must, to our roots—

        alert for any signs of prey near the surface—
            'As when a cast of Faulcons make their flight
                At an Herneshaw that lyes aloft on wing'.

Time our foe: breath whipped by wind and
        heart like a foolish old sheepdog lying down or
                running or hopping at intervals for a few feet

and at last still. All senses, eyes, ears, stretch
        to the next listening point beyond the horizon. Calm
            in late afternoon light. Attention slipping away

      ' hunger in all weathers '

            Throstles feeding—
                            hunger
in all weathers—
              on the ground   the crops

        stand stiffly upright.
                    Head
cocked to one side, a fisher
                alert for signs of prey

        a ripple
            near the surface
betrays it.
        Running or hopping or

    at intervals still
        and silent
—attend
    for a few feet more the earth

    —snail to anvil—
         attend
to the next listening
     point

Committee

Throstles feeding—a savage committee down
on the ground in anger. To stand
stiffly upright in that storm of nerves, a politician's
head cocked to one side in dishonesty.
Alert for signs of prey they hover

near the surfaces of our lives to tear them—
running or hopping, breathless beasts scramble
at intervals into our lives. No pity—
for a few feet of earth tied by our ears
to the next listening point—forever.

Tankers, roofs and pittance

Tankers docking at the Grain refinery may have to wait hours
standing off in the fast tidal waters of the Thames Estuary,
their sailors watching lights of Tongue, Midbarrow and the coast.

Stars on a partly cloudy night appearing, disappearing,
their distance infinite. Seen between old pine trees
on top of a hill fort, they seem at once abstract and human.

The small town with its sharply sloping roofs, its old walls
crumbling, with swallowtails basking on them. Four people wander
together in the sunlit streets. And the first swallows returning.

Throstles feeding stand stiffly upright, head cocked to one side,
alert for signs of prey near the surface, running or hopping
at intervals for a few feet to the next listening point.

Lead spoil-heaps fringed with spring sandwort, harebells, remains
of old workings. Once so many people toiled here to take ore
for pittance wages. Tried to eke a family living from the earth.

Homage
to W.C.W.

thrushes
feeding
on the
ground

stand stiffly
upright
head cocked
to one side

alert
for any signs
of prey
near the surface

running
or hopping
at intervals
for a few feet

to the next
listening
      point

Kalangaeaf!

Winter—all afternoon the throstles feeding
on windfalls which lie on the ground

amongst dead annuals—their stalks stand stiffly upright
beside the path. The old cat, head cocked to one side,

watches us from the wall, alert for signs of prey
or passing enemies, or goldfish near the surface

of the small ornamental pond. Running or hopping
or getting under our feet, a dog follows at intervals

down the path—you walk on for a few feet
beyond the roses, to the gate, to the next listening point,

where we must part.

Alternate

    Against the odds   throstles
  feeding on snails   eager after rain
     the ground   dark and wet
where a few plants   stand stiffly upright.
  Breathing deeply   robin's song
    head cocked   standing alone
to one side of   the path   alert for
movement   rising moon   and clouds
wind signs   to us, waiting   owl hunting
in far wood   sounds of prey   grounding
  near the edge   the surface dwellers
running or hopping   or making their cries
  under skies   still torn by clouds
  at intervals.   Leave the garden
walk down this track   together with me
  for a few yards   so many years
  our feet together   our breath
    together   to the next
      listening
       point

Stars on a partly cloudy night

Throstles feeding—their neighbours basking in evening light
on the ground, or in midgy air, or by puddles. Teasels & hogweed

stand stiffly upright, in moral purity, listening. A terrier,
head cocked to one side, awaits his call. Moon is an owl, rising

alert for signs of prey, combing the copse low over beechwood,
near the surface of the undergrowth. Heartbeat racing—animals

running or hopping or standing or lying down. The moon
at intervals caught behind cloud—a planet in step with us

for a few feet as we go home—too tired and breathless—to
the next listening point, hearts spinning like toys to the sky.

Larksong Signal

Arcane and isolate breathing
acts of faith—longstone
to blind fiddler. High song
patient in rain. *Sing it—*

no ideas but in tunes—
'sounds we haven't heard
that the birds know about'—
writing on air for dear life

Messenger

unknown and unknowing. Dancers
jiggle to warm in their hive, its

stray parts—song—multiplied in the
chimney's veins, season colours on blue. Thief

of my heart, as ever—you my
life, my heat. *Learn'd to play when he was*

young, and still 'meanings now
not in words, but in air

around them'. Always so.

for Ann 14/2/99

Milkwort

Worker in metal.
Place it like a charm
under skin.
Close to ground.

Against fear.
Against ill-health.
Against riches that blind
my eyes to riches.

Motive

    these fields, slow
        driving
  home, cold
      sun

Nine Englynion

The Ash Tree That Bears Apples
– Nennius

Glad it was so: not pushing for reasons
      or easy answers, just
   happy to walk down the path

with winter sun in our eyes and ears cold
      from wind, pushing branches
   from faces; no need for words.

Late afternoon, the world turning to night
      its last light weakening
   low in branches: bitter fruit

Tenebrosa Sicut Nox

Days dark as night, can't work, can't sleep tonight,
      my glass and book empty;
   eyes dim, my mind on small things.

Light low, I sit up in the gloom tonight,
      witless, I write little,
   pale thoughts weighing my blind brain.

House quiet, white frost, a sinking peace: tonight
      my mind is in the east
   in set dark: my fears grip tight

The Coat

Where to look for it? Frail light, far at sea,
        a land frost set as salt
    wind's temper fretting our steps.

Going alone: breathing hard on the cold
        to break it, fear like a
    starbeam on the path, dark faith.

Finally casting it off. Song lifting
        and going on alone
    in frost, the same and yet changed

Parsley

Evening: smell of parsley
thinned in late May after rain

Poem For My Mother

The piracy of thought
                from memory
becomes real
in winter—poor birds
        their weight is lost
        and they fall
—here too a voice
                maybe called out
in the night   unanswered.

There were no words.

Someone wrote a poem called 'The Trees'
dancing   unheard
out of their leaves
—not still.   Poem not heard.
                Trees too noisy—
                boughs crashing
                      wrenching twigs
birds dashed down.

She held my head
while I sicked   the garden
at night   rich
unresting   where she sent
my mind
        she cooled
my head.

Helpless words—
there is no song

```
    but this        the tumult
    of our love
                still
    too loud
            and real.


    She was
    never still.
```

Ramsons

a calm, a
    red sun low
in my driving mirror.
    pale moon.
smell I can't drop, or
    song, chance, wild
garlic, a weather
    beaten sail

Rigmarole: And Each Several Chamber Bless

          Long time coming:
the music a
    shattered column of
       light splintering
           on curtains
       knife point salt
on tongue—
    forget night—
       forget stars—
          forget motor-
       fret, the sea
the air, the closed
    door, breath
       curdled on paint—
          many ways, a
       long time coming
of doubt—little things
    being crushed under
       big wheels of
          days—of thought
       not being clear—of
iron shards picking out
    light like
       the stars. The flowers—
          they were small and free
       and they could
stop the machine
    with hope
       with splinters of light
          with telephones—
       the roads were
dark and breathless
    windows of pale gold all
       summer night under
          trees and steady

                        thrum of the tide,
long time coming—
        love, panting
                white with
                        silly stitchwort and
                        ramsons, the splinters,
the lips, the hair,
        salt.
                Many ways
                        of love, not
                being sure, never
losing balance or
        sense of loss
                of balance—kick
                        the door, it
                never closed or
opened and probably
        wasn't real anyway
                like freedom. Then
                        turn out my pockets
                look for the
green pencil stump,
        cloudbank, hankie,
                life triumphant,
                        my heart, my

                eyes, finding
in it after all
        a place
                for the genuine
                        long time coming, a
                song of the high
hills and everything
        fading away
                before it. So
                        trees blossom and
                birds nest and
bob up and down

so hard, their
> comic act, their
>> real need
> to be alive
a voice
> in a room
>> at night
>>> longing, not
>> learning more
than the fond eye
> doth teach, a
>> frame of pale gold
>>> air shifting over
>> owls, pewits, lorries,
everyday
> no more
>> than is needed.
>>> And many ways
>> splintering light
birdsong, balancing
> being in love
>> and holding it
>>> like a flame
>> we who hold the planet
and the smell of it
> hits us.
>> Only being alive
>>> is left, it's been a

> long time coming
we called for it
> like the psalms
>> and then we fell,
>>> in love. There are
>> flowers, stars, and
many ways.

> Magpies and jays.

Rigmarole: A Struck Bell

roofs cluster darkly babble . embattled
I work here . we breathe and sweat
voices never still . I must draw out .

        root   bleed
        silence   thought

choose pitch and tone as vegetables .
heart . & so tosses & turns .
to blue sound on the edge .

        the owl   the eagle
        & the blackbird

from heat mist on a spiral . bedraggled
& fighting . against dark power
what shall we play ? a wind harp .

        root   silence
        thought   bleed

harsh straights of border conflict .
a busy bustling . out of traffic flow
within an ivie todde

        the owl   the eagle
        & the blackbird

tossed & torn . twittering of birds everywhere .
cars everywhere . what shall clean it ?
rage of the surf driving

        root   thought
        sulphur   bleed

ayre ybroken . buildings in moonlight .
tattered & ragged with great coat tyed in strings .
fancies within a literal age .

        the owl   the eagle
        & the blackbird

cursd critics . rubbed the stone clean .
weeds are dressing murmur .
absent in movement

        silence   thread
        root   bleed

routine . the trap that is called distance .
turning a book . *I made a song in a murderous time .*
must return to silence .

        the owl   the eagle
        & the blackbird

raven sound of wave on stone . in the night .
I must breathe . carways gasping .
moths plop into light . brackish .

        silence   root
        thought   bleed

the sun dropped . clamour of turning wings .
phrase in the night . I wish my neighbours wilder .
dictionary .

        the owl   the eagle
        & the blackbird

written and erased alone . in dark
inherent memory . days work praises itself .
to draw on . struggle . roof pounding

        silence   thought
        breathe   root

alone . neither music nor politics .
the colour of daybreak on clear sea .
my own voice comes to me as a struck bell .

        the owl   the eagle
        & the blackbird

Rigmarole: Block Quilt
for Ann

scrape the vellum   wipe the disk
ready to be anything
or sat down at stone table in frost
patchwork concerns

nearly crashed the car   surprised
by cornflower   blue splash   a character
in early morning traffic   care for you
and for small memories in lost context

not that you asked for a poem
curled asleep   insight of mountains
to place such pieces   spirall roundles...
conical sections, circular pyramids

stem pulled into breathing   repeatedly
clarity of thought   capture of brindled ox
capture of cauldron   escapers
storming the glass castle

mind anyhow morning   backchat
in the kitchen   vegetables found
at the bottom of the sea   ready
to be anything   over and over

breaking bread with   light   patterned
memory   tight chested   air
beyond thule   thick condensed and gellied
mountain air you could bite

or how spots of persicaria do manifest
themselves between sixt and tenth ribbe
fallen long ago   we greet ourselves
from our separate thoughts

body falling into its own absence
common range   a shoe-leather handshake
recalled   lose the file
curling asleep under an old steep roof

branching off from   hanging onto
tom saying 'socialism's not dead'
and a tenderness comes to it
snow on the mountain tops   driving

with a cold certainly makes me nervous
cato seemed to dote upon cabbadge
scrape the record   into the common range of
humbleness   each to its windy niche

living backwards   one of those characters
with a hand like a boot   weeding
all on the bare moorside   had been forested
merlin   bright-eyed in frost   forgotten

land foundered   wading out alone
a bog path, cottongrass-covered   rods and sails
sleepers in brushwood   a sub-marine herbal
ready to be anything   lasting to world's end

a long line flowing   bottle of wine
got broke   things left in sand
stitch   upon stitch   morning
and parting   over and over

was mad in the dark forest
since destroyed   breakfast
visible things   the song come down to us
or else forgotten or mauled or put aside

in a world when small   body falling
out of dreams   yellow   cream and
white on black   patient
rhythm of the cave   lost songs

lost upon fading into the autumn
patchwork   a fine concern for pattern
recalled   facing into the hills at dawn
vanity, feeding the winde   having no

grace of speech and so shamed
obliteration of the fact   the past
repeatedly   you could stand firm
on a grassblade   magpie words wideopen

finally and unasked-for   caring's not dead
written on the margins of sleep   speedwell
stitchwort, gentian   a distillation
eyes open and so much to learn from them

it's what remains   when the slate is wiped
just wanted to say   I love you
and all of this too   pieces laid side by side
for clarity   no easy way

of breath   no wasted effort
the songs finding themselves   curled asleep
miles away   escapers in tender
common range of visible things

Rigmarole: Night-Driving In Corrèze
for Lucy

Night air
   a little
ahead
   of
night itself—
   look—
light
   falling
behind us.
   In what
are we
   and by
what
   charm
bound? O
   daughter
bright as day
   and curious—
in clear air
   memory lightly
calling to us—
   but hard
—*immortal hand*—
   wind
we drink
   like water
striking
   our hearts.

Our hands
   to lizard eyes—
warm in

   those parts—
wall
  nooks of
creeper old
  blackbird
castles black
  bright
quick
  darting
run—a hunting
  animal
call in
  those woods—
'hunger
  in all weather.'
Rock walls
  washed
with brown
  ores—
blood
  residue like
poor wine:
  sharp on
the tongue—
  taste—dark
wind of
  night coming.

Rivers, coldcut
  deep in
their gorges—
  and we
watching them—
  as what
ancient people
  watching

and sensing
    this place.
Who painted
    deer   horses
on the rock's
    curve—alive—
with what
    wondrous grace.

'Long ago'—stories
    told and a
tune piped
    by firelight—
a hillsong—
    headlights
catching on
    woods,
dark sticks.
    At each bend
your head
    falls
a little; curve
    of your neck
(car mirror)
    a pattern
reflected   I'm caught
    soft on it.
Bats and
    little owl
seen in trees—
    small animal
shapes   sounds—
    driving
our light
    defines us
—*forests of the*

  night—
cornering
 tired
towards sleep.
  Hard breathing
in night air
  our thoughts
surround us.
  Never still
and with us.
  That you
drink it in
  as new—
you laugh,
  are ardent
in what you do.

  I love you
for that, too.

Rigmarole: The Dogs Of Vilnius

    the
    dogs of
    Vilnius—
        tongues
    lolling over
    teeth—*we were*
    living on another
    table—
        and this
    is the thin
    corn ear an

        entanglement
    of aural
    perceptions
        arising
    into new grace, or *let*
    me be sick
    myself

        voices rising
    and falling
    in language
    you don't
        understand
    —with their
    tails
        sweeping
    the ground
    nother full
    greene, nor
    full
    yelowe

   & each one
alone—yet
included—as a
charm
  against
forgetfulness
running
across waste
ground or
looking to the
stars in
  rain

   the dogs
of
Vilnius
neither old
nor young
urbane in their
mobile phone
  foraging—
robbed by
harsh chance—

anger
  running
from the jaw—
an idle syntax
   —I wonder
how we might
replace
earth's nourishment

  grasped
the rise and
fall

of the
speech
notes
        —roots
of a political
anguish—or
how we
mourn
a mischief too
old to
tell

the dogs of
Vilnius—young
in an old language—
one tea and
a tall beer
        leaning
back in their
chairs—
the tale was how
cross she was
wouldn't listen
for anything
        against
dark buds of
vines
        plastic tables

        to bring
words out of
the dark—margins
reach down
each gateway
        barking

        & neither wild
        nor tame
        nor fast
        nor lame
              you reach into
        damp mist—alone—*be what*
        thou singly
        art

the
dogs of
Vilnius are
wideopen—
willing &
never still—
our practice of
selective
       chance
in morning's light
     magpie
     voices—

a sweeper
with a twig broom
sweeping along the
four lane
motorway
—no kidding—
why I feel the
sun burnt through
     every
word—at
sea's edge,
these were
the windes,
unto

        which it
was well
exposed,

city, forest and sea—
        a borderland—
I do not come
with a
language—
of regret

the d.o.V.
—tired, tired
children lost in a
profane age
        —well,
it had rained
all day
the traffic
        poisonous
as if
        you
wanted to
hold me
but were
afraid to
let
        go, be
caught in
night's
channel—*swim*
smoothly in the
stream of thy
        nature

muzzles
serious, saying
  at last
you know
what
I mean
it's music
it's sound
business
  you

hold the line
hack & slash
for the
Genitive
  case

and go
laughing
sniffing
late spring
  flowers
like wine
when
everything moves
transparent
the will
stays
the same

the dogs
of Vilnius
  wishing
it could be
otherwise
  alone
& in pain
at their end

Rigmarole: Uncertain Time

flag-
    stone rocking on unstable
base, the rain

    gone under it,
sunken puddle. A speech
    at odds with itself, as

likely to
    soak you as save you.
Ann's voice

    clear out of the kitchen *I must
be going no
    longer staying*—shapes

that delight
    and try us. Rocking
the stone

    under pressure—now
Keys of Canterbury pulls
    the mind along—in songtime

in balance. For instance
    if one could understand a flower
in God. It's rained

        all week,
clothes won't dry and when we do walk
      it's buttoned up (flag

tips a little)
    nothing but the plants—cow parsley—
make it

    spring. Dark politics surround us
at odds
    with time—a child's hand

draws us—
    once I had a sprig
—I stumbled

    when I saw
voice, steps
    little gusts, plants, things

we love in balance.
    Heart. As
likely to soak as save you. Fail,

    fail if you
must but in terms you are
    helpless

within, her breath
    any colour when finally the rain
stops, the line clear

        and in tune, time
is fulfilled when time
    is

no more
    the pavement tips as you move
your foot — wet

    through.

Shelter

The motion of
                a section opening in
click
you saw me?

The motion of a door
                    opening out
it's just trees
around the frame, through

the frame, the boundaries
you set yourself, disappearing—

You're there—
that 'humble dwelling'
maybe needs painting—   limits
        of the known world

she comes to the door
with a child

'It is all that is made'

The motion, finally,
              of veins
opening under the hill, slowly,
patiently   sound
          of the ores
being formed.

Little Stringer

Milky stem   ragwort breaks up
out of the soil
         we can use

follow the veins
         your wits
woolgathering
follow the veins

heavy leads   out of the hills
waters wash them away
the rains   the simple course
we use   follow
the veins

Lichen days
light   a
         history—

I have seen the hills and they were just the hills
I faced into the wind, it blew on me

rest there—

Hitting the Vein

The day I terminated my lightning-fast mustard gas liaison with catholicism was also, 'by chance', the first really rainy day of the autumn 1977/78, with its inherent discoveries of torn coats, leaky shoes and lost slates.

I became, after this, a firm believer in the workings of chance—a belief which has since been shaken.

    Hazlenut

    The thrush ...
    is preening the lawn

    rain
    flattens my allergy
    my heat
          distemper

    this world, Mother Julian

    ... and the wren   (recap)
    'It is all that is made'

        the bird
        flits

        the grace
        notes

Interlude: Where did that dog get in?

The trees

'gone for lunch'

they have panned ores
from these streams
all summer

the giant pumps are turning

a large shaggy spaniel (?springer)
rests in their (implied)

shade

Nothing certain
          for Tony Lopez

Afternoon: sun south
                the south wind blows
thin soil
landfalls cover the plough

The motion of eye
          shutter

```
         falling
         woodrot        to powder
```

```
         Now I watch pigeons
         wheel into light—
         the hedge is now
                         isolated
         trees by the track
```

```
         dust      grit     snow-in-summer

                         wind
         out of sun blows
         nothing so certain
         as my views

         change
```


Metal Poison

Tonight the city oppresses me: constricts my chest: separates me from my loves. Incessant machine tension, the streets threatening.

City sky never dark: red clouds retch over me. The motors run all night and the people who would have them run live far away. Like many I spend my working day far from my wife and child, often get home too tired to care for them: I try not to resent this, and fail. For now I make this small counter-equation: small-scale ontological reinvestment for all the family. It scarcely seems enough at times.

Streets gleam: before me, in the dark, a wind brings me a taste of the moisture of trees.

Sweet Receipt

You care for me   together
we go shopping
                get the food
                go for a walk
(the prince rode to that castle
            long ago)
you, me, Tom.

Work hard /
            no time
last night
you were sad
and cried to me
my breath tight

we get so tired

The feast still on the table
the storybook lies closed—
         I care for you, I
         really do

See stars through
holes in the roof
thoughts crashing in
to turn to you

Already the kitchen staff were waking

The Limits

A street, a burnt cat.
destroyed shelter, storm cloud
on the town.

Vagrant.

North.

Dutch doll blue sky night and fear spreading

☆

Lamp   firelight
she sews

a quilt

☆

Clear moon
frost held tight
the field

and further out
the town
       lies locked

my thoughts edge
on you

Smithy

Memory's forge—you
just stood there
in the street, the sun
still above you.

Harebell on ridgeway—
a fallen tree
to sketch, you just
standing there in heat.

Sweet Cicely

song: sweet cicely: history

That scent.
        The Queen
rode out at daybreak
past the white flowers.
They nodded. It was
May, these were
hard times.

She held
        her head
high through those
rank grasses.

⚔

All
the little things:
        that found thing
        bright
as Annie's eyes
are brown.   Share

sun : eyes : hands

    this gift calm
    beyond possession
    gift of love

※

sweet cicely

    As simple. To move there
    like the birds.
                  To breathe
    That scent. Wind

    blows off the town,
    off nowhere.
              O be *local*
    at times rife—
    the sweet assurance
    the foot kicks
              where it will

    be loved
    and alive.

※

A catch
breath shrinks

past firelight
dusk over hills

and beyond
cool

flame on vision

We are off from it and our words
smoulder
   in mayweed smell
   no ownership
   common arrest
     (no revolt)

we part skyline
brother fire
   our minds
are fuel.

   Pace out
heart on
throat (beat)
   gentleness
of the phrase turned up.

   (The song is twisted into the grass
   which snatches your ankles).

song: left handed sickle

You are as ignorant of your beauty
as the day
        we met. You bend
the grass we push through.

You are free and sharp
and vital to me
as the day.

The hard compromise
(through my bonfire's smoke
the last marigold
unquenched)
of pushing (winter)
aside
the dry stems
to be lost
in pipe dream
music
on Observatory Hill
mist on city
ache
of wind song

heart
in its silence.

Light gone
from the dales
and stars
lock in.

⚹

As held
new leaves in
lamplight:
         little moves

blessing
to stand still
to make spell for weather
to be loved
feel air on face

o sing—

         switch-
       grass of liberty
        breathless

       hedgerow pressure-
          drop pulse
          cloudbank
           stirring

—how we are changing as the tides

✠

                              song: the dance of morning

the heart of a breeze
the hope of plants
the shock of coffee
the rhyming of birds

the grace of clouds
the meeting of hands
the dance of morning
the mark of rain

✠

A
fall
of
notes
as
apple
(engine)
mist, a
first
hint of
winter
    shed the dust
air
opaque
tree
driven
parts
arise (half-
seen)
    heard
in the
lull
of traffic
    (never)
heart
    to heart
to ear
stone (worn)
in the air
the pact
    you
and I
    sometimes
remember
    to make
each year

The Feet of Dafydd Ap Gwilym Tapping to the Triads of Dr. Williams

i

Yesterday
under
the trees

waiting
for
a girl

haunches
of
a fox

ii

O quick
brown
fox glance

flowers
chain I bound
am bound in

the web of
the shame of
my lacking

tongue

iii

Alas the clock
    wakes the ducks
churlish clock

    drunken cobbler
treacherous hands
    to mock

light
    in a girl's
arms

The Paths

Two converging from
night, household
sleeping—moving
so together:

here a dipper
there a stream
here a pillow
there a dream.

Three Reels
for Ann, in advance of a valentine

'The Pretty Clippie'

The dance of cash,
our hands
will never meet—

this stage—
this night sea's loose
breakers change—

this (sprayborn)
delicate commerce
of streetlights

'Caddel's Favourite'

We move
together. Out of
night's quilt

with air and cloud
and times
constant pressure

whose will, cold head,
we'll
weather.

'The Chippy's Still Open'

Bootheels—appetite
hitting
the wet floor

of rhythm. Echo
distant tripwire,
snared light—

to catch street power
and draw desires
foothills.

Two Movements Which Begin at the Head and End at the Feet

Autumn / Dowland

As my mind's leaves
are blown
in tiny piles

so these airs
fret at their sense—
the foot is a pace

behind the song, the song
behind the wind
wind teases the leaves

across the bar
to fall
at my feet

Spring / Purcell

Eggshell is the
mottled view my
windows give, my

fingers and my
wit : the street is
leaves birds' notes

drop from. Night is
calm, still—
the song of the moon

to the feet

Uncertain Steps

Not, I
    said pushing
back

    bushes from
Ann's
    face and

the kids'
    that
there's a

    gap—
here's
    the path

between
    content and
comment—look—

    the orange
hawk-
    weed by

that burnet
    rose—
mind

        your feet
Ann said
    if you're

going through
    there—I
did—the

    warm
smell of
   water-

mint
    hit me—planting
my foot

   on
it. The print
   of my shoe

in mud—
   it's
gone

now.

Underwriter

blocked morning—I bite
my day and swing out
over sound, over

the past, over blown pompous
lifequake up high
and out astern. Building

great names of light
painting out, over
tired out heart—

writer
drowning in space
in planets ache

it's weird—night in your eye
and text-frame, nose
into unsure silence

below Stonypath Ltd.—full
ships' stores in everlasting. Come
buy your stars anyway

here gripping the stone of winter
here underwriter stalling
in sound over coppice.

Fallowfrost print on
the week, so glib, nothing but
moonlight forgotten out there.

And glibly on common way
over stubble the scarf the
waymark unstill

over sleepingsickness
over turf of the law hear
heartsong down morning

✠

horsehair viola bread—
chaff in the bright morning—
bread broken asunder

✠

the blood root aloft there
in wind light—irridescent earth
warm and lime washed

big grasp of urban door open
an apple house in song
mother or summer or clear

blue edged with blood all
softened in winter wood mind
coldsilver

wandering each day of
esoteric signs—sound
gesture into the dirt lands.

Or loving being born or
thrown to the flood over
alley over flood over care—

your poems flung in forever
dazzle—the twofold
heartabsence—

contract on the world gone on
nights kiss hard against
speech, signpost

to waking homeless
in unnatural street clothes
a scattered sky

salt caked robed in its rime
the paint the plaster the ship
the hope ever silent

in Darien—you hanging
your heart filtered out
your kinfolk—light,

light in showers foundered
our sound singing in
fruitless ache. Memory

cranks up astern in
untidy never still legend, lover
you fled from, your parents, your

passage creature painting
bent feet alive stops your
wet starsight forever

⚔

for Tom, 10/2/98

over all your days
grief—your being
to yourself elsewhere

unmeaning world—your
damage in a thousand words
lost, lost of worth such

as our verb lover wore for
his sister—this veiled
glass array lost

in words that might soothe.
Farewell dark sluice must
ache: speech in the saltflood

flicker noise remembered
today in its innerlight
absent

✠

dark wine and spilled
by snow — I rode
the sea sound you

lost, military fern —
never-never war song
on lying herd. Bitter. Open

your fireducts leaving
in liquid line
over gardens green as so

written so
crying into their so
wrathful prebuilt words

✠

out of silence: here fell
here metal rail not here
management facesaving

sour prayer—here their bit-
event crippled tongues.
Here shame

out of their meanness
your stem cut
honour flaming—

and you—you forever
caught on that time law
of roses where were paths.

Their crude dis-
honesty of words: childsong
turned cold heard

without heart—eyes fall
watchful wherever tear
over tear stops

dank. Moss-trooper
of mass, bring-it-home
anthems of unending

light wider
in dawns and draughts—
drinker of portent sans

therapy-led dish-out of
tumult—you're stark
and starker. Thank

you, to your own hand
with a wide
inner love

unbearable earth glittering
hardon. Thinking
so dusk comes out

of your name your hand your
inner fire
unquenchable

⚔

for Lucy, anytime

clean night winning my
hinny, honey, limning
your light over powering

all the sound starmantles
all the half might
all that wasn't lost falling

⚹

held in these stones:
our left lurch held
wide light of strangers

and swollen night gardens anew
new stars, new
troubles—sighing out

and wringing briar rose
scented so sprightly, you
my lease life on world.

I say so. You pull with my
heart, my
harbinger each boulder you turn

in bright again wine
in rough song its
grey night of no naming

⚹

of warm human. Postnatal
thief in glowing
absent script timelocked

small birds from the air you
hear down—a
mutt-in-the-moon—down

✒

whosoever. Round grabber
groundless in strict time
go year written off.

Starlight rings washed
breathing my memory
bassoon solo o' my heart

crushed. Where light
stole into our days
oilgreen and salt

stippled against
centre-grey stone against
bitter seated dock

forestorm, its
wounded
brilliance. Child

standing may painted
whosoever on night sea
invading your mind harbour.

No air, no voice, reader-
eye feelings smart
good night each trembling

page. Go grass script
nocturnal by or from printed
estuaries

✠

true search in foxlight
and you, where to fit
you in. Out of

a shine sky living heart
minus warmth, well-
being and moon swelling

thinly to starglow—I touch
the quick grey stolen brush
hold its surprise fast

✠

for Ann, 14/2/98

the nest empty, that
speaking, neat green
bird-in-bush

in flood love season
a moon drawn out
sent tumbling

forever anywhere—here
in editorial over-
singing cut-and-paste

where in shutter green
absence, your real
sound shines out

Vers Nègre

My black self. Another
has me, monkish.
A second moon, paler,
gleeful, further

across the sky, and I
a child, listening.
Silence. Another
has my life.

Writing In The Dark

**5 CAREER MOVES NEGOTIATED IN THE DARK
ON A BACK STEP IN NORTHERN EUROPE**

Pavier

This heavy slab. Our memory,
tone of our plant life trained
to go round it. Beat
it out and we pulse

together, it's a wonder
we don't rave daily. Whack!
Whack! go another's
psychotic dreams, the sad

sky path we all must walk.
Light goes, it does, *now*, so
stars show, us under them,
breathing, apart, blessed.

Crystallographer

Sky at night, who can fathom it?
We all can. A chinese
smile takes me out of myself, these
downers lifted by shining

my teeth, jumping in planetary
time. If you love me
you love its *sound*, this faint breeze
and its eternal traffic noise

vibrating. No need for gods, we
breathing this age daily
and after all this time
the shapes we sense are new.

Distiller

The deep throb of cello. Water
becomes us all, our
starry selves. That we could
lose so much and still

live. 43% proof is pure
belief, clarinets below the
surface of our breathing—*in*,
and *out*. Memory will

drop from us but never
completely. Snuff this
dark varnish liquid, life. We
love it. Let it go.

Florister

Young girls laugh in the lane, a word
like that giggle doesn't exist.
Out of a lexicon of reedy days
release this pavement of colour.

Supplier: here is a thirst, a bloom
lightness blown past me
to the stars, won't be quenched. And a glass
slab to keep us from forever.

So long, so longing, violin tone and
spirits to breathe
together, these young colours
tied and gathered in a bunch.

Trucker

Traffic noise silent. We listen
awed to plopping of heavy stones.
Thunk! Blockaded as we are, we drink
extemporary horn solos as we

sit out late with sinal and dental
headaches. Here's a flower
we'd all forgotten, from a pot
marked nightmare. When we're

finally tired, we sleep like children. So
breathing it reaches at last
to an argued form of blessedness, a
silvered road deep to stars.

6 VESSELS ENCOUNTERED IN THE DARK
IN SPACES BETWEEN EAST AND WEST

Whaler

Hard times then, and blocked
with blubber. We sailed
with Captain Heartsease
on the old *Starlight*, kind

sirs I could not tell it all. Stand
firm and hopeful, O lookout
of the night. A trickle
accordion, and an old pump

fit to bust. And every word is
true, each planetary body
so old, every ache reminds us
of home, forever set about with salt.

Planter

This bindweed—everywhere—my
heart in treetops, fruit
strangled by its flowers. *Dangerous
passage, ahoy!* At night

we sniff exotic scents, small
trees begin to dance for us.
We make our world with love
and care, want it looking

the same from each direction
but it can't, and weeds
are named one by one. We
speak and ask too much.

Dipper

In night—a water-drip rhythm
made from need, sweaty
as can be and more so. That
we love and it runs away—isn't that

all of it? Bitter mouthfulls
cry it to distant stars in black
and long for it. There's a way
of saying so that no hurt

takes: *parsley*. But that's
not in this starry maths.
We step back from it all
dog-tired. Hedge crickets sing.

Charmer

Simple water. *Bright water.*
Heavy water. It runs down
glass outside while we stay
talking, talking our days

away. Then we wash down
those strange stars, and gardens
everywhere lose their quiet.
Come and have food. Then

be still beside me and
don't talk in this dry night.
Wooden forms polished. Grey
light loved in your hair.

Lighter

By starlight on a clear night
insects sing, a music apart
on margins we thrill to. Leaving
presents we can't leave. Kind.

Made sounds always answered—
Bamboos bending in wind—
heartbeat to a friend's pulse
in aching times, breath

under moon, and *the journey
itself is home.* Wideopen.
With thanks for this new naming—
clear singing light.

Condenser

World made small, a
temple garden or
ice bag on cheek bone.
In radio chase night

we are one, alone. Our
needs, our
loves. Stumble away
from it. Be

yourself. Breathe easy
under star music.
What you believe
is true.

Wyatt's Dream

Whose eyes were sleepbound and
whose song stilled
saw the blade a bright beam
cleave the shield.

His love walked from the grave
veiled. Songster, fighter and
lover stilled.
There in the cave.

Notes and Acknowledgements

Any writer publishing extensively in small magazines and presses incurs real debts to the people who make up that exciting and shifting world. In my own case, the debts to that community are considerable, and happily acknowledged. But failing memory and incomplete filing have left me with a sketchy publishing record for some of these pieces, and what follows is liable to be only a partial record. Some of these poems, then, or versions of them, first appeared in the following magazines, anthologies, broadsides *or others*—and if the instigators of those others would care to jog my memory, I'll be happy to thank them publicly on a future occasion. To all of them, my thanks.

Alive in Parts of this Century: Eric Mottram at 70 (North & South 1994), Angel Exhaust, Boxkite, *A State of Independence* (Stride 1998), Atlantic Review, Colorado Review, Denver Quarterly, Conjunctions, Figs, *For John Riley* (Grosseteste 1979), Fragmente, Gare du Nord, Giants Play Well In The Drizzle, Great Works, Grille, Jacket, Kite, Landlocked Press, *Louis Zukofsky, Or Whoever Someone Else Thought He Was* (North & South 1988), Meanjin, Molly Bloom, *Motley for Mottram* (Amra/Writers Forum 1994), *The New British Poetry* (Paladin 1988), New American Writing, Ninth Decade, Northgate Press, Notre Dame Review, Object Permanence, *Other: British and Irish Poetry since 1970* (Wesleyan University Press 1999), The Paper, Perfect Bound, *The Poetry Book Society Anthology* (Hutchinson 1991), Poetry Durham, Salt, Scripsi, Shearsman, Slug Press Broadsides, SubVoicive Poetry, Talisman, *Voices for Kosovo* (Stride, 1999), West Coast Line, Writing.

Special thanks are due to the following individuals who've published sections of this work as pamphlets or collections: Tony Baker (Figs), Andy Brown (Maquette Press), Kelvin Corcoran (Short Run Press), Michael Farley (Taxvs), Tony Frazer (Shearsman Books), Harry Gilonis (Form Books), Randolph Healy (Wild Honey Press), Peter Hodgkiss (Galloping Dog Press), Peter Quartermain (Slug Press), Ian Robinson (Oasis), Peterjon and Yasmin Skelt (North & South), Tod Thilleman (Poetry New York).

This selection is intended, as I've said, for readers rather than scholars (the two groups are distinct in my experience). I've therefore kept notes to a minimum, seeking only to account for terms and structures without which a reader may be left floundering.

A SHORT CLIMATE-ATLAS OF THE SOUL
One of only a few exercises in cut-up which I'd wish to preserve. The source material includes Gilbert White's *Natural History of Selborne*, and *The Ladybird Book Of Weather*.

COUNTER
The formal structure celebrates a number of works on the dance-language of bees, and diseases of the blood. The Themerson quote comes from *Bayamus* (1949) and translates as 'Young-brother again / Son again / Hereafter I-shall / See never'. The Schwerner is from *The Tablets* (1999). The first was published in the year of my birth, the second in the year of my 50th birthday.

FANTASIA IN THE ENGLISH CHORAL TRADITION
A fantasia is a loosely-structured piece allowing for elements of formal development. I acknowledge here my debt to the English choral sound, from its beginnings to the present, and to the resonating of the human voice in ecclesiastical space.

FOR THE FALLEN
A reading of Aneirin's *Y Gododdin*, this is taken from A.O.H. Jarman's edition (1988). It is done in memory of my son Tom. The three sections reflect, roughly, three methods of 'translation':

1-39	selective literal translation
40-75	loose phonic translation
76-100	free palimpsest rendering

It is unlikely that any of these approaches would satisfy a scholar of Old Welsh.

GROUND
My *Ground* is a modified approach to the musician's understanding of the term; musical terms tend to acquire extra meanings in the course of translation to literary use. E.M. Nicholson's attempt to re-instate some of the older names of common birds (see, for instance, *Birds and Men*, Collins, 1951) was lost in a sea of pesticide. No ground is pure.

LARKSONG SIGNAL
Nearly all this short poem is derived from quotation in some form or other, but the quote in quotation marks is from African composer Obo Addy.

NINE ENGLYNION
Englynion penfyr from the book of Llywarch Hen, together with the shorter of the two Juvencus englynion, have been very much in my mind when writing these. Purists may object—justifiably—that I have been too free with this three-line verse-form: I hope it's obvious that this was my intention.

RIGMAROLES
The OED describes rigmarole as 'incoherent; having no proper sequence of ideas; rambling'. For me a Rigmarole is an exploratory form made of the sounds of words: rambling only in that it must find or negotiate its form; coherent within its own terms, as research projects might be. All my Rigmaroles are quote-heavy and make use of structure repetition. At the back of my mind too there is an older definition of rigmarole, from Elizabethan street slang, as a piece of cant, or a repeated trick phrase or quote, used to gain admission.

UNDERWRITER
Although this work began as a group of phonic translations, it progressed so far beyond these origins, burying them irretrievably in the process, that it's no longer appropriate to acknowledge them.

WRITING IN THE DARK

Some (rare) fine evenings in England, and others in Japan, together with a hand-held Psion with a backlit screen, enabled me to sit out late and make the initial notes for these poems literally in the dark. As a methodology, it is, obviously, an exploratory one, with a nod of homage to the title of Robert Duncan's last work. The series is ongoing.